THE FUTURE IS FEMALE

ALTERNATOR BOOKS™

T0018885

Changemakers in
ACTIVISM

Women Leading the Way

DR. ARTIKA R. TYNER

Lerner Publications ◆ Minneapolis

To the Honorable LaVune Lange, global leader and changemaker

Lerner Publications Company
An imprint of Lerner Publishing Group, Inc.
241 First Avenue North
Minneapolis, MN 55401 USA

For reading levels and more information, look up this title at www.lernerbooks.com.

Main body text set in Aptifer Sans LT Pro Medium.
Typeface provided by Linotype AG.

Designer: Athena Currier **Photo Editor:** Nicole Berglund
Lerner team: Martha Kranes

Library of Congress Cataloging-in-Publication Data

Names: Tyner, Artika R., author.
Title: Changemakers in activism : women leading the way / Dr. Artika R. Tyner.
Description: Minneapolis : Lerner Publications, [2024] | Series: Future is female | Includes bibliographical references and index. | Audience: Ages 8–12 | Audience: Grades 4–6 | Summary: "Women have always made their voices heard. From historic to present-day women, young readers uncover changemakers who fought for their rights, took a stand for the environment, and much more"— Provided by publisher.
Identifiers: LCCN 2023022629 (print) | LCCN 2023022630 (ebook) | ISBN 9798765608838 (library binding) | ISBN 9798765624975 (paperback) | ISBN 9798765618226 (epub)
Subjects: LCSH: Women—Political activity—United States—Juvenile literature. | Women political activists—United States—Juvenile literature. | BISAC: JUVENILE NONFICTION / Biography & Autobiography / Women
Classification: LCC HQ1236.5.U6 T96 2024 (print) | LCC HQ1236.5.U6 (ebook) | DDC 320.082/0973—dc23/eng/20230411

LC record available at https://lccn.loc.gov/2023022629
LC ebook record available at https://lccn.loc.gov/2023022630

Manufactured in the United States of America
1-1009545-51561-6/22/2023

Table of Contents

INTRODUCTION

Advocating for Change

On June 19, 1968, fifty thousand people marched in the Poor People's Campaign in Washington, DC. Activist Marian Wright Edelman helped create the march to show the struggles of people with low incomes in the US. Protesters wanted better jobs, housing, education, and more.

Not all the protesters' demands were met. But Edelman didn't give up. She kept organizing and created the Children's Defense Fund. The organization tries to make sure that children have essentials such as good food, health care,

Wright at the Children's Defense Fund in 1987

and education. For over forty years, Edelman's organization has helped thousands of children.

This book profiles female activists such as Marian Wright Edelman who have made a difference in the world. There is not enough room in these pages for every woman activist. But the women featured here are dedicated to leading change in their communities and inspiring others to join them.

CHAPTER 1

Standing for Environmental Justice

Some activists speak up for the environment.
They want to take care of Earth so everyone can enjoy it.

Helping Chimpanzees

Jane Goodall studied chimpanzees. She made many discoveries about them including how some were being hurt at research facilities. Goodall saved chimpanzees from these places.

Later, Goodall went to a science conference. Many people were talking about deforestation, or removing trees in an

Goodall watching a chimpanzee in 1987

area. After the conference, she saw how much of chimpanzees' habitats were being lost to deforestation.

Goodall gave speeches around the world to tell people more about chimpanzees and the dangers they faced. She also raised money to protect them. Goodall founded an institute named after her that helps chimpanzees. She also created a youth leadership program.

> **"What you do makes a difference, and you have to decide what kind of difference you want to make."**
>
> —JANE GOODALL

> ## "Kids need to see themselves as superheroes."
> —MARI COPENY

Fighting for Clean Water

At eight years old, Amariyanna (Mari) Copeny made her voice heard. In her town, Flint, Michigan, the water was unsafe. Lead from the city's pipes was going into the water. Lead can harm people, especially children.

In 2016 Mari wrote then-president Barack Obama about her city's water crisis. Obama wrote back and visited Flint. He later sent $100 million to help fix Flint's pipes. In addition to money from the government, Mari raised over $250,000 so people could have clean water. Mari became known as Little Miss Flint.

In 2019 Mari helps give people clean water.

Mari continues to speak out about the water in Flint. Some pipes have been replaced. But as of 2023, some Flint residents have gotten infections from drinking the water. Mari wants everyone to have access to clean water.

Standing Up for Native Rights

As a member of the Mississippi Band Anishinaabeg Nation, Winona LaDuke fights for Indigenous rights. While in college, she advocated for ending uranium mining on Navajo land. This mining released toxins that could hurt people near it.

Later, she helped fight to have land returned to the Anishinaabeg people. The US government had gone against a treaty with that nation and sold land to companies. The Anishinaabeg lost the lawsuit, but LaDuke kept speaking out.

LaDuke wants Native peoples to control their homelands, natural resources, and cultural practices.

Thunberg at a Fridays for Future protest in 2022

Friday Protests

Fifteen-year-old Greta Thunberg was worried about climate change. So in 2018 she started a protest. Every day she stood outside the Swedish parliament to get them to act. At first, Greta was alone, but then others joined her. Greta's protest moved to every Friday. Her protest spread to other countries.

CHAPTER 2

Making a Difference in Education

Education creates many opportunities for people. But not everyone has access to it. These activists are working to change that.

Building a Legacy of Hope

Mary McLeod Bethune was a lifelong educator. She believed in the importance of educating girls and preparing them for leadership roles in their communities. She started her own school where young Black women learned reading, writing, and life skills.

Tearing Down Barriers

At just eight-years old, Sylvia Mendez tore down barriers in education. She and her siblings were not allowed to go to their local public school because of their race. They were told that they could only attend a school that was for Mexican Americans. Sylvia's parents filed a lawsuit in the 1940s against the public school and three other school districts and won.

Mendez receives the Presidential Metal of Freedom.

Sylvia attended the public school. She went on to become a nurse and speak out against segregation. In 2011 she was awarded the Presidential Medal of Freedom.

Creating Access to Diverse Books

Eleven-year-old Marley Dias loved reading. But she had trouble finding books about Black girls like her. She launched the #1000BlackGirlBooks drive to collect books about Black girls. Marley donated the books so people could read them. She spread her message on social media. She has collected over thirteen thousand books and even wrote her own book.

Marley speaks at a protest in 2020.

STANDING FOR EQUAL RIGHTS

Marjorie Bell Chambers championed women's rights. She wanted to pass the Equal Rights Amendment. This would make sure people were treated fairly regardless of their gender. She spoke out about the amendment. She advised several US presidents on women's issues. As of early 2023, people are still trying to pass the Equal Rights Amendment.

Chambers (*left*) speaks with President Jimmy Carter and adviser Sarah Waddington in 1979.

Champion for Girls' Education

Malala Yousafzai was eleven years old when she found out she couldn't come back to school. The Taliban had taken over

Malala keeps speaking up about girls' rights to education.

her city of Swat Valley, Pakistan. Malala spoke out about girls' rights to education. When she was fifteen years old, someone shot her for speaking out. Malala recovered and continues to let her voice be heard.

"Some people only ask others to do something. I believe that, why should I wait for someone else? Why don't I take a step and move forward? When the world is silent, even one voice becomes powerful."

—MALALA YOUSAFZAI

CHAPTER 3

Leading Change in Health and Wellness

People's health impacts their everyday lives.
These activists are raising awareness and taking a stand for causes related to health.

Working to End Gun Violence

After surviving a shooting at her high school in Parkland, Florida, Delaney Tarr knew something had to change. Tarr cofounded March for Our Lives, an organization made up of young people working together to stop gun violence. She

Tarr talks at a March for Our Lives rally in 2018.

helped organize one of the largest marches in Washington, DC. Millions of people attended to protest gun violence.

Raising Awareness about Autism

On August 24, 2018, a crown was placed on Karyl Frankiewicz's head. She had been selected as Miss Native American USA for 2018–2019. Throughout the competition, she brought awareness to autism. Autistic people have different experiences with it. But it can be expressed through close attention to detail and sensitivity to lights or sounds. Frankiewicz was diagnosed with autism when she was eight years old. After her crowning, people thanked her for talking about autism. She continues speaking up for herself and others.

PROMOTING SELF-LOVE

Jameela Jamil (*below*) wanted to create an accepting space on social media. So she created the campaign I Weigh. It promotes self-love and says people are more than their weight.

IMPROVING HEALTH WORLDWIDE

Barbara Bush (*below right*) is training the next generation of leaders. She is the cofounder of Global Health Corps where she works to address the most challenging health-care issues. Bush and other corps leaders are working around the globe to promote health and well-being for everyone. She has been named one of *Glamour* magazine's Women of the Year and *Newsweek*'s Women of Impact.

Advocate for Disability Rights

Johnnie Lacy refused to back down. As a Black, disabled woman, she faced discrimination. But she kept speaking up

RAISING AWARENESS ABOUT BREAST CANCER

In 1982 Nancy G. Brinker founded the Susan G. Komen Breast Cancer Foundation to support breast cancer research, in honor of her sister.

against racism and ableism. She cofounded the Berkeley Center for Independent Living in 1981. This let more people with disabilities live on their own and have more freedoms.

Lacy helped people with disabilities live more independently.

CHAPTER 4

Speaking Out on Politics

Women activists play an important role in making laws and policies. They use their voices to fight for justice.

Protecting the Rights of Immigrants

At five years old, Sophie Cruz made her voice heard. She was born in the US, but her parents were undocumented immigrants from Mexico. She was worried her parents and other immigrants would be deported. So she wrote a letter to Pope Francis. The pope is the leader of the Catholic Church.

Sophie addresses a crowd in 2017.

When Pope Francis was visiting Washington, DC, Sophie gave him her letter. The pope was impressed with her letter and talked to Congress about immigration reform.

Using Music to Inspire a Generation

Joan Baez used her musical talents to make a difference. She wrote and sang songs about things she was passionate about. Her songs focused on people's rights. She protested for civil

INSPIRING YOUNG PEOPLE TO VOTE

Yara Shahidi (*below*) founded WeVoteNext. The platform encourages young people to vote and get involved with the issues they care about.

Baez performs for an audience in 2019.

rights, worker's rights, and more. She founded the Institute for the Study of Nonviolence. It stands up against injustice.

A Voice for Equal Rights

Yuri Kochiyama experienced discrimination and wanted to make sure no one else did. She spent two years in an incarceration camp during World War II (1939–1945). After an attack by Japan, President Franklin D. Roosevelt signed a policy that forcibly removed people of Japanese descent in the US from their homes and sent them to incarceration

In 2004 Kochiyama looks at a memorial for Japanese Americans who were incarcerated during World War II.

camps. Kochiyama also stood with the Black community during the civil rights movement. She attended protests and sit-ins, made flyers, and wrote newsletters to help draw attention to the movement.

Advocate for Children's Rights

Madonna Thunder Hawk is part of the Oohenumpa band of the Cheyenne River Sioux Tribe. She stands up for the rights of Native Americans. She is a tribal liaison for the Lakota People's Law Project. Grandmothers who sought to keep children safe and protect their rights founded the project.

Thunder Hawk watches a movie about Native rights in 2019.

She also helped to develop the Simply Smiles Children's Village to bring together Native foster families. She founded the Wasagiya Najin grandmothers' group on the Cheyenne River Reservation to bring the community together.

Spreading Kindness

Lizzie Velásquez stands against bullying. She has a rare disease that prevents her from gaining weight. People bullied her for her appearance. She speaks out against bullying and encourages kindness.

Velásquez speaks in front of a crowd in 2018.

CONCLUSION

Changing the World

You can also be an activist. Discover what causes you care about. Then you can get involved. You can tell other people about your cause, make flyers, or start a club about it. Then you can help make the world a better place.

You can make a difference by talking about causes you care about.

Glossary

amendment: a change in the words or meaning of a law or document

discrimination: the practice of unfairly treating a person or group of people differently from other people or groups of people

environment: the natural world

foster: to provide care for a child when a parent cannot

government: a group of people who control and make decisions for a country, state, or other political unit

health care: prevention and treatment of illnesses by clinicians

immigration: moving to a country to live there

lawsuit: a case before a court of law to end a disagreement between people or groups

organization: a company, business, club, or other group that is formed for a certain purpose

policy: an official set of rules or ideas about what should be done

Source Notes

7   Jane Goodall Institute, accessed April 12, 2023, https://janegoodall
    .ca/what-we-do/#:~:text=Jane%20Goodall%2C%20has%20
    famously%20said,believe%20in%20for%20a%20generation.

8   Allison Klein, "10-Year-Old 'Little Miss Flint' Helped Hundreds
    of Underprivileged Kids See 'Black Panther' over the Weekend,"
    Washington Post, February 20, 2018, https://www.washingtonpost

.com/news/inspired-life/wp/2018/02/20/10-year-old-little-miss-flint
-helped-hundreds-of-underprivileged-kids-see-black-panther-over
-the-weekend/.

15   Brian MacQuarrie, "Malala Yousafzai Addresses Harvard Audience,"
Boston Globe. September 27, 2013, https://www.bostonglobe
.com/metro/2013/09/27/malala-yousafzai-pakistani-teen-shot
-taliban-tells-harvard-audience-that-education-right-for-all
/6cZBan0M4J3cAnmRZLfUmI/story.html#:~:text=%E2%80
%9CSome%20people%20only%20ask%20others,even%20one
%20voice%20becomes%20powerful.%E2%80%9D.

Learn More

Britannica Kids: Marian Wright Edelman
https://kids.britannica.com/kids/article/Marian-Wright-Edelman/623403

Britannica Kids: Winona LaDuke
https://kids.britannica.com/kids/article/Winona-LaDuke/635394

Jones, Amy Robin. *Mary McLeod Bethune: Pioneering Educator*. Mankato, MN:
Child's World, 2021.

Kiddle: Marley Dais Facts for Kids
https://kids.kiddle.co/Marley_Dias

National Geographic Kids: Greta Thunberg Facts!
https://www.natgeokids.com/uk/kids-club/cool-kids/general-kids-club
/greta-thunberg-facts/

Neuenfeldt, Elizabeth. *Greta Thunberg: Climate Activist*. Minneapolis:
Bellwether Media, 2022.

Schwartz, Heather E. *Malala Yousafzai: Heroic Education Activist*.
Minneapolis: Lerner Publications, 2021.

Tyner, Dr. Artika R. *Changemakers in Government: Women Leading the Way*.
Minneapolis: Lerner Publications, 2024.

Index

Photo Acknowledgments

Image credits: Cynthia Johnson/Getty Images, p. 5; Penelope Breese/Getty Images, p. 7; AP Photo/Jake May/The Flint Journal, p. 8; AP Photo/Chad Harder, p. 9; JONAS EKSTROMER/Getty Images, p. 10; AP Photo/Charles Dharapak, p. 12; Elsa/Getty Images, p. 13; AP Photo/Mark Wilson, p. 14; AP Photo/Julia Nikhinson, p. 15; AP Photo/Andrew Harnik, p. 17; Marla Aufmuth/Getty Images, p. 18; Abaca Press/Alamy, p. 19; Courtesy of The Bancroft Library, University of California, Berkeley, California AV Project (cabeuroh_000258), p. 20; Theo Wargo/Getty Images, p. 22; AP Photo/Omar Vega/Invision, p. 23; Debra L Rothenberg/Getty Images, p. 24; AP Photo/Mike Wintroath, p. 25; Foc Kan/Getty Images, p. 26; Rich Fury/Stringer/Getty Images, p. 27; Klaus Vedfelt/Getty Images, p. 29. Design elements: Old Man Stocker/Shutterstock; MPFphotography/Shutterstock; schab/Shutterstock.

Cover: AP Photo/David Niviere/Abaca/Sipa USA; AP Photo/Ashlee Rezin Garcia/Chicago Sun-Times; AP Photo/Chris Pizzello/Invision.